I am Kept

Extracts from Diary and Letters of a young
soldier of Christ in Bank, Billet and Battle-field

Charles Harold Mawson

Scripture Truth Publications

First published 1918 by The Northern Counties' Bible and Tract Depôt, 63a Blackett Street, Newcastle-on-Tyne.

Re-typeset from the Seventh Edition with additional notes and transferred to Digital Printing 2017

Centenary Edition October 2017

ISBN: 978-0-901860-54-5 (paperback)

Cover photograph of wild poppies and wild flowers at dusk, Flanders
©iStockphoto.com/MikeMareen

Published by Scripture Truth Publications
31-33 Glover Street, Crewe, Cheshire, CW1 3LD

Scripture Truth is an imprint of Central Bible Hammond Trust, a charitable trust

Typesetting by John Rice
Printed and bound by Lightning Source

"I AM KEPT"

Extracts from Diary and Letters of a young soldier of Christ in Bank, Billet and Battle-field

HOUSEHOLD ———— BATTALION

THE NORTHERN COUNTIES BIBLE AND TRACT DEPOT,
63R BLACKETT STREET, NEWCASTLE-ON-TYNE.

Original cover

Charlie Mawson (1898-1917)

This Booklet contains brief extracts
from the Diary and Letters of

TROOPER

CHARLES HAROLD MAWSON

(1527, HOUSEHOLD BATTALION),

of Whitley Bay, Northumberland,

who passed into the presence of the Lord,

AT POELCAPPELLE, N.E. YPRES,

OCTOBER 12th, 1917.

Aged 19 years and 8 months.

"Where the Saints in glory thronging,
Where they feed on life's blest tree—
There is stilled each earnest longing,
Satisfied our souls shall be.

Safety—where no foe approaches;
Rest—where toil shall be no more;
Joy—whereon no grief encroaches;
Peace—where strife shall all be o'er."

John Nelson Darby (1800-1882)

I AM KEPT

Foreword

Several years ago, as I was researching biographical information on J T Mawson, I was made aware that extracts from the diary and letters of his son, Charles, who was killed in action at the First Battle of Passchendaele during the First World War, had been published posthumously in 1918. Reading them, I fully shared the delight that Handley Moule experienced as he read the manuscript before contributing his preface.

As Charlie muses on his desire to be totally committed to following Jesus Christ: first at work in a bank, then in military training and finally in the thick of battle in Flanders, I find his writing truly inspirational.

100 years have passed since the day in October 1917 when Charlie, as a shell burst near him, went to be for ever with his Lord and Saviour, no longer to be found on earth. His name is recorded on Panel 3 of the Tyne Cote Memorial to the Missing in Zonnebeke, West-Vlaanderen, Belgium; but, as he himself said of other believers, "How splendid to leave the army…with a record…in the Lamb's Book of Life." His story is a challenge to us all: in these more settled days, do we face our problems with the same uncompromisingly cheerful faith as Charlie faced his?

John Rice
October 2017

Original Publishers' Notice

We are more than thankful for permission to publish these extracts and the portrait of the Author of them. We specially pressed for the latter because we feel that his many friends would be glad to have it incorporated in the book.

The story the following pages tell is at once a striking testimony to the grace and power of God, and a source of encouragement to many Christian young men in similar circumstances.

We ask for a wide circulation for the little book, and count on God to use and bless it.

THE NORTHERN COUNTIES' BIBLE & TRACT DEPOT,
63A, BLACKETT ST.,
NEWCASTLE-ON-TYNE.

Prefatory Letter
From the Bishop of Durham

Auckland Castle,

Bishop Auckland,

May 12th, 1918.

My dear Sirs,

To-day, in London, on a quiet Sunday afternoon, I have at last read *"I am Kept"* from end to end.

As I closed the book, I found myself speaking aloud, though alone, a heartfelt thanksgiving.

To me, in these tremendous days, when not only death and grief are so thick around us, in the great conflict for mercy, liberty and truth, but when it is almost as if "all things" were "coming to an end", and the very Gospel seems widely forgotten, it is inspiring and cheering in a wonderful way to read Charlie Mawson's diary and letters. I bless God for this splendid young life, filled and used, first in peace, then in the fiery crucible of soldier-life, not by any vague "new thought", nor worship of mere manhood, but by the old and unchangeable Gospel of the Grace of God in Christ.

I bless my Lord for the message brought to me by this young believer, who, like Hedley Vicars[a] long ago, "burnt his boats", let himself be "a marked man" (while never forgetting that the "marked man" must be the bright, unselfish, simple-hearted comrade), and found the reality of the promised "keeping power" alike in Bank, Billet, and Battle-field, and so left a radiant track of light behind him.

Charlie Mawson is indeed not dead. He lives with his Lord above, and he lives as His Witness here in these bright pages.

You have done well to produce the beautiful booklet, with the portrait, eloquent of purest and bravest happiness, for its frontispiece. God give it wide circulation, and follow it with blessing to every reader.

I am,

Yours truly,

(Sd.) HANDLEY DUNELM[b]

The Publishers of *"I am Kept"*.

Introduction

When, under the "Military Service Bill", the call came for the young Author of these extracts to join the Army, his exercises took shape under three heads—

(1) His obligation to submit to the higher authorities under which he had been set in the providence of God;

(2) If he sought relief from these obligations his bit of the burden would probably fall upon shoulders less able to bear it;

(3) If a sacrifice of life were called for, the Christian young men who were ready ought not to hold back.

He was sent on October 25th, 1916, to the 2nd Life Guards, and put into the Household Battalion, headquarters at Windsor, and on his first night there he fully realized that if he was to be kept from being swept away by the tide of evil he must be "out and out" for Christ.

That the Lord answered his earnest desires in this regard comes out in a letter from the Lady Superintendent of the Soldiers' Home in Windsor, under date February 6th, 1917. She wrote to his home:

"Your boy scarcely ever is absent from the Home, and I am sure his mother and you would rejoice to know what a whole-hearted lad he is, and so *untouched* by the defilement of army life. He is a dear lad, and full of love to his Lord. He gave us a little message to-night after two other Christian men had given a word of testimony."

The diary was written for no other human eye but his own, and left behind when he joined the Army, and had he lived none other would have seen it. The later extracts are from letters written, with three exceptions, to his home from Windsor and France. They appear as they came from his pencil—the simple and free expression of his experiences, and heart's desires, especially sacred now to those who received them, and only published because of the assurance that they will be of help and encouragement to many Christian young men in His Majesty's service and elsewhere.

Diary Extracts
— working in a Bank

"Just as I am—without one plea,
But that Thy blood was shed for me,
And that Thou bidst me come to Thee,
O Lamb of God, I come."[1]

I have been too greatly blest of God to be a worldling ...
How longsuffering God has been to me. O God, let me
come to Thee, to be Thine alone! Am I a stone that I can
accept all these good gifts at Thy hand and be unmoved?
Cleanse me, O Lord! I deserve that the wrath of God
should abide on me alway. But there is no good to Thee if
my soul goes down to the pit. Save me, for Thy mercy's
sake! Make me a Daniel in Thy things! Lord, give me to
love Thy word. Give me a hearing ear and an
understanding heart!

How proud and self-satisfied I am because God has given
me health and strength and a sound mind; but if I look at
myself as I really am, how much greater is my
transgression than that of those around me? O God, give
me grace!

"Oh, the regret, the struggle and the failing!
 Oh, the days desolate and useless years!
 Vows in the night so fierce and unavailing,
 Stings of my shame and passion of my tears!"[2]

But on, on, on. *Nil desperandum.* How should one with such a God ever give up hope?

"So to Thy presence get me and reveal it,
   Nothing ashamed of tears upon Thy feet,
 Show the sore wound and beg Thy hand to heal it,
   Pour Thee the bitter, and pray Thee for the sweet."[2]

Truly it is better not to be, than to be and not be noble. *What then is true nobility?*

"Incline my heart unto Thy testimonies, and *not unto covetousness.*"

God in His infinite mercy has been shewing me my own nothingness. "In me, that is, in my flesh, dwelleth no good thing."

After such a talk as I had last night with — —, I feel I must seek the Lord more earnestly for guidance and wisdom and grace. Time is short, and we are so weak. But blessed be His Name, He is so gracious!

Came home cast down because of slips made at my work towards end of day. I must pray about this more. I believe God is speaking to me in my work at the Bank. I want to be a real Christian, in everything devoted to Him. Lord help me! Save me from myself. Keep my eyes on the goal, and may I plough a straight furrow.

O Lord, give me great faith! Thou art my strength! without Thee I can do nothing. Help me this day, O Lord! Help me in my work this day! In my work, O Lord, help me this day!

O God, I come to Thee now in my youth to serve Thee and to be Thine all the days of my life, and shouldst Thou give me length of days, then may I be able to say at the end of them, I have served the Lord from my youth up.

My business is to find out what God would have me do, and DO IT, as if there was nothing else in the world.

Let my life be what it ought to be, a song of praise to my Creator and Redeemer!

Why should I wish that men should think well of me? If I am honest with myself, I have to confess what I am. Why, then, should I desire that others should put a different estimate on me?

The thing that counts is that which is done for God, whether men are pleased or not.

May the Lord help me to be just and true and kind in all my dealings with my fellows. Life is a serious business. No life can be right, and no one can know true happiness, apart from HIM.

May I not seek the flattery of the world, nor the good opinion of men at all, but may my watchword be, "I serve the Lord Christ."

Big Zeppelin raid last night. Went out and watched the blaze. What insane folly this kind of thing is! And how true is Romans 3.15-17[†]. I pray that I may have wisdom how to live in these dark days. "Thou wilt keep him in perfect peace whose mind is stayed on Thee." Indeed, the Christian has a goodly heritage. How blessed to walk in the joy of it; and say, "He waketh me morning by morning."

Nothing should prevent a man getting into the presence of the Lord before going to the day's duties.

While I yet live may I not live in vain.

> "Can it be true the grace He is declaring?
> O let us trust Him for His ways are fair!"[2]

Military Service Bill passed by a great majority. Of course it does not come as a surprise. But I do wish that I had spent more time in prayer about it, then I should have been clear and decided about my own course of action.

This will be one of the greatest changes that will happen to me. I do not know what lies before me. I must put away from me all childishness, and must think and act as a man—not of the world—but of God.

> "Fearless in the fear of God."

What shall I render unto the Lord for all His benefits towards me? Well might I ask such a question. Nothing will do but the absolute surrender of my life to Him.

> "Christ alone can save,
> Break the power of sin;
> Christ doth fully satisfy
> The heart that trusts in Him."[3]

The Christian who means to live to the Lord must have no worldly friends except to win them for Christ. He is in a measure responsible for them. How hard it seems to me, so sensitive as I am, but I can do all things through Christ that strengtheneth me. Praise His Name! Oh, grant wisdom and courage, and may I be imbued with the power of the Holy Ghost. "Let him know that he which converteth a sinner from the error of his way shall save a soul from death, and shall hide a multitude of sins."

Be careful in the little things of life. No self-indulgence; be good-natured to all. Nothing can be done without earnest prayer and the study of God's Word. Why is it not valued more?

A— and C— must be brought to a saving knowledge of the Lord Jesus. I am responsible for both of them.

God has given me good health and strength; may they be held altogether at His service.

"He that hath knowledge spareth his words" (Prov. xvii. 27). He does not speak rashly, unadvisedly, or unthinkingly. He weighs his words and considers the possible effect of them. He does not babble on uselessly, vainly. Therefore is the man of knowledge a man of few words compared with the fool.

> "Not many lives have we, one, only one.
> How earnest should that one life ever be,
> That narrow span."[4]

> "And life is all the sweeter that he lived,
> And all he loved more sacred for his sake,
> And death is all the brighter that he died,
> And heaven is all the richer that he's there."[5]

What beautiful lines! How glorious to have them in some measure true in my life. Then why not; look well to it; thou hast the opportunity.

… To be strong, fearless, kind, calm, helpful, honest, unaffected, earnest, quick, thoughtful.

Make no allowance for yourself, but every allowance for others.

Cease from debate and betake yourselves to be alone with God.

God has blessed me in every way.

O God, for strength, for courage, and for calm. I pray that I may live as one that serveth Thee.

"He hath showed thee, O man, what is good, and what doth the Lord require of thee, but to do justly and to walk humbly with thy God."

Abraham had the heart to choose and to prefer God, and to venture for Him and for the will and call of God before all else in the world.

"What think ye of Christ?" That He is the Son of God. MY Lord and my God.

Oh, that we understood the highness of our calling. Then should we be kept from things common and mean. May I live in the light of Christ's glorious appearing!

Mine must be a life of service and prayer. ... I have put my hand to the plough. Oh, may He keep me from looking back.

"Thou wilt keep him in perfect peace whose mind is stayed on Thee." Remove far from me vanity and lies. Lead me on, that I may live for Thee alone.

It is not sufficient for the Christian to live what is called a moral life, every beat of his heart must be towards his Lord. How careful I must be in my bearing towards all, even the greatest stranger, for who knows what may result from a kind word.

What a fine man Duncan Matheson[c], the Scotch Evangelist, was. Like the Apostle Paul and all who serve Christ absolutely, he was entirely forgetful and careless of his own comfort, and worked like a slave; but what a glorious bondage!

I bless the Lord for the past, praise Him for the present, and put my future entirely into His hands. Lord, make me a man of prayer.

To sleep with thoughts of His goodness and to be awakened by His touch, feeling the need of prayer and communion with Him!

Lord, humble me before Thee. Let me be a servant of all. Put away from me all my sinful pride.

In bed at 10.0; up between 2 and 3 for a solid hour in prayer in the still night watches.

> "I gave My life for thee,
>   My precious blood I shed
> That thou might'st ransomed be
>   And raisèd from the dead,
> All this I did for thee;
>   *What hast thou done for Me?*"[6]

Remember, "dead in trespasses and sins", or "risen with Christ".

Got my wages to-day. All must be consecrated to Him.

Only a few short years, and then eternity—ETERNITY!

How anxious we are to gain the good opinion of others, and how strangely careless as to whether we offend the Almighty God!

The men who separated themselves to David (1 Chron.‡)—

> "They were fit for the battle.
>   Their faces were as the faces of lions.
>   They were swift as roes upon the mountains.
>   They had understanding of the times.
>   They were not of double heart.
>   They could keep rank."

From Letters while Training
— Billeted at Windsor

Got to Windsor all right, and am now amongst the Life Guards. We are an active service battalion, and so shall not get any frills. I was looked up and down by a keen-eyed Captain and then examined by the M.O. With a mild expletive, he said, "What were you doing on an office stool with a physique like that? I should like you for the Horse Guards." That cheered me up, for I was feeling a bit ashamed of myself.

S— had got your letter and found me out and took me round to the S.H., where we had a sort of Bible Class. Very nice.

I think that joining the army has been to me a great blessing in disguise. Difficult, unpleasant, and altogether uncongenial it often seems, but through it all one's own pride is shattered, and great becomes the desire to know the Lord as the Friend that sticketh closer than a brother.

> "His arms are round about me,
> How can I be dismayed?"[7]

I have thought of late of W— and L— a good deal. How splendid to leave the army not with a D.S.O. or even a commission, but with a record such as they have, not on the army conduct sheet, but in the Lamb's Book of Life.

We must put away from us all fear of man, and do what we think is most pleasing to the Lord. What a glorious faith is ours!

I am more convinced than ever that I must give up my stripes. I am giving it, you may be sure, full consideration, for it means much to me, for before I joined up I always told my friends that I was keen on promotion. But now—

> "Content to let the world go by,
> To count no gain or loss,
> My sinful self my only shame,
> My glory, all His Cross."[8]

Here is a fine hymn, with a swinging tune. (774 S.S. & S.)

> "One little hour for watching for the Master,
> Eternal years to walk with Him in white;
> One little hour to bravely meet disaster,
> Eternal years to reign with Him in light.
>
> Then, souls, be brave and watch until the morrow!
> Awake! Arise! your lamps of purpose trim;
> Your Saviour speaks across the night of sorrow;
> Can ye not watch one little hour with Him?"[9]

I know that many of the Lord's people remember me, with other young Christian men, in their prayers. How greatly blessed we are, and how readily we ought to yield up our lives to Him. But continue to pray with increased fervency that I may grow in grace and faith, for the darkness around is very deep.

On Wednesday I spoke here on the concluding verses of Romans viii. I find that speaking to others is a great help to my own soul.

I do desire more than ever to serve the Lord with my whole heart. And do continue to pray for me. I generally find that after an unusually precious day the devil comes in and tries to trip me up, so that there is the constant need to watch and pray.

I can assure you that I need to keep home memories very close to me, for army life has a very dark side. How dark, few civilians can even guess. ... I thank God every night that for 19 years He kept me in an atmosphere of love and Christianity.

I cannot get home yet. We have just begun musketry practice, and it is an unbreakable law that no one goes on leave while on this course. Cheero!

> "Every step of my onward way,
> I'll sing, He knows, He knows."[10]

I do not care to speak of my deeper spiritual exercises, but I know that you are constantly praying for me, and will be glad to hear how God is answering your prayers.

You will remember that in November, 1913, I was greatly exercised after that long walk and talk we had, followed by Mr. W—'s meeting at B.G. It was then that I saw what a blessed thing it was to devote all one's little life to the Lord's service. I prayed earnestly for a long time that I might be made a useful servant in the great Gospel field, if it was His will, and that I might walk worthy of Him. I could not count how many times I have prayed over Ps. 51.

After a time I got discouraged and seemed to lose interest, but always felt in my heart that as God was true to His promises I should have an answer to my prayers, and so in a way was ready for it when it came. Since I joined up, not suddenly, but slowly and surely, I have felt that He was answering them all, mine and yours too, and my one desire is to serve Him faithfully and fearlessly in the place where He would have me be. With the increase of this desire my old shyness has gone. I have confessed Him before my comrades, and I am a marked man. It is a great joy to feel that I have burnt my boats and that there can be no turning back.

> "He knows the way He taketh,
> And I will walk with Him."[7]

The Army is a fine training ground for a Christian. There are so many things to jar one's temper, and you are always in the presence of other men who watch you closely.

There is an "R.C." in our room; he said to-night before all the men that meeting me had changed his character. No one swears now in our room, but it is difficult to make men understand.

Rather an amusing incident the other night. I was in bed with my eyes shut when the corporal came in and began to row a man. He said, "Old Charlie's asleep, so I can swear at you." He laughed it off when I told him I wasn't.

The "R.C." went with me to the S.H.'s and accepted a Testament, and took Collett's "Scriptures of Truth".[11] I thought it would help him, as he questioned the Divine inspiration of the Scriptures.

On Tuesday the class consisted of fourteen youngsters. It was quite easy to tell them of the Saviour's love to them. On Sunday I was asked to help in the Gospel Service. I left this with the Lord and knew that He would guide aright. It gave an opportunity of speaking to my chums; one of them was with me, and I had to tell them on what authority I stood up to speak. How easy it is to speak of the Saviour when we leave all to Him, and don't forget that in us there dwelleth no good thing.

— was telling me about the —. ... This does not bother me at all. I am where the Lord would have me be. As to promotion ... I shall just continue one of the happiest troopers in His Majesty's Army. Pray for me, that I may be KEPT, and so no dishonour brought on my Lord's name by any conduct of mine.

On Sunday I went round one of the billets with some notices of the meetings at the S.H. The men thanked me and accepted tracts. I am getting plenty of opportunities for service, and the Lord is helping me.

— went back to France last night; his turn at the front seems to have made him a bit callous. — will get a commission. It is when talking to fellows like these that the old Adam rises, and the old world pulls hard, but daily my desire to be kept unspotted from the world increases.

I have thought much lately of how greatly my way of life has been changed. From a beautiful home—how beautiful it seems to me now, far away—into circumstances of constant trial and never-ceasing contact with sin and wickedness, which, as you told me before I joined, does make itself most prominent in an army of men—yet through His grace KEPT happy and strong in Him.

How blessed it is to be a Christian! The days are far too short, and I am always sorry when it is "Lights out", for I have no idle moments. I am afraid that I have too easy a time of it here, everybody is exceedingly kind to me.

I was asked last night to speak to the mothers of the children who attend the S.S., and was only too glad of the opportunity of saying a word for the Lord. A young Christian, who is in the band, went with me and played the harmonium. We had a good time. To-night I had the Young People's Meeting, and after it had time to get round to the S.H., and got in a few words there before we closed up.

So glad to hear that your friend of the train journey was really converted. His story was so interesting and encouraging, that I told it at the Home.

The Lord is very good, and though often tempted and failing, yet I can say I AM KEPT, and my desire after Divine things increases. My heart goes out hourly in thankfulness to God for His goodness to me. I hope I may be able to do others good.

Of the future I can calmly say,

"I am not skilled to understand
What God hath willed, what God hath planned;
But I do know, at God's right hand
Sits One who is my Saviour."[12]

"My bark is wafted to the strand
By love divine,
And on the helm there rests a hand
Other than mine."[13]

I am glad you noticed the word KEPT in my letter. I thought you would do so. I am reading the life of

Brownlow North[d]. In it it is remarked that he always put in his letters, "I am kept."

The more I consider my position in the army, the more I find to thank God for. It is quite clear how His hand has been lovingly and gently guiding. I am quite contented, and am learning that godliness with contentment is great gain.

Yes, I'm a number too, and a very happy one, because *my name* is in the Lamb's Book of Life. You, too, seem to have got into a fine Training School. How wonderfully the Lord looks after His own. If we leave ourselves in His hands He can use us, but not otherwise, dear comrade in His service. *(To a friend)*

The great thing is to keep an unfrayed and cheerful temper, and have a smile for all comers, and all day. May God help me!

I am very deeply touched by the news that — has been killed, and have written —. Yet it is so difficult, I should like to have quoted some lines from "Sleep on, beloved!"[14] and yet how could I? How sad it is, and how earnest it ought to make us in our desires to win the souls of those we know for Christ. How different the death of a Christian friend would have been, and what a consolation a Christian parent has about a Christian son.

> "Thou art gone to the grave,
>   but 'twere wrong to deplore thee,
> For God was thy ransom, thy guardian and guide;
> He gave thee, He took thee, and He will restore thee,
> AND DEATH HAS NO STING
>   SINCE THE SAVIOUR HAS DIED."[15]

To the dearest and bravest little Mother in the world. We were warned just half-an-hour ago to parade at 9-50 a.m. on Sunday, to proceed over seas. I shall have time to run round and say "Good-bye" to the kind friends in Windsor, and clean up my pack and put it together. I have got your nice letter. … I have had a very very long time in England, and looking back on the 7½ months of training I have few regrets, and can look forward to what the future may hold quite calmly and happily. All I want to know is that you dear ones left behind are facing your trials, which I know are greater than mine, as happily as I am. I have not had to report sick all the time I have been here. You will be glad to hear that.

My very dear Father. Very many thanks for your letter. I shall not forget my Bible. I was at Mr. D—'s last night, and had a long and helpful talk. I am sure the Lord will look after me wherever I go, and I do trust that you will not have an anxious thought about me. I should have liked another Sunday here, but it is not to be.

My very own sister. Don't pull a long face when you get this, my sweet child, for I shall have lots of time for letters when I get across the water. What an adventure! I wonder how soon I shall be back to see you all again.

My darling little M—. By the time you get this I shall be on my way to France. Fancy you having a big brother in France! I should like one big hug before I go. Can't they send you by parcel post? Lots of kisses; hundreds of them.

Everything as jolly and nice as can be. Nice day yesterday. Got to bed at 11.45 p.m., after putting my pack together. Dear old pack, it does make you straighten your back! Slept like a log until 5.0 this morning. We fell in on the square at 9.45, just as if we were going to an hour's drill.

Then the Colonel came: "Dra–aft! 'Shun! Well men, I wish you all good luck and God speed." Then the band struck up, and led us through the 1½ miles of street to the L.S.W. Station. We were all happy and smiling as we swung along, pouring out sweat, for it was awfully hot. We were allotted to our carriages and then allowed to talk to our friends. The D—s were there, and Mr. P—. It was all great fun. Quiet fellows in my compartment; discipline is perfect in the H.B.

From Letters from France — on the Battle-field

I got into conversation with a nice Christian sergeant in the Rifle Brigade. We had tea together in the Salvation Army hut, and stayed to the Service. The room was full; about 150 men. The S.A. people are very emotional, but no doubt do much good here. It was nice to see the men listening, anyhow.

As I lay on my back in my D.O. at 10.30 p.m., wrapped in my overcoat, for the nights are chilly, I began to ponder the events of the day. It had been a glorious Sunday. Almost the only variety in the deep blue above had been the puffs of shrapnel smoke, and indeed, unusual aerial activity. I was wondering if it portended anything for us dwellers in the earth. I did not wonder long. The Boche began to pump a storm of shells into a position behind us. … They whizzed and banged and screamed, according to their nature, over our heads. I did not trouble to look out. An extra loud crash, and I thought to myself, that some day, if the war continues, I am almost certain to be under such a fire as some poor fellows are enduring at this moment; and thinking thus, I smiled a little sadly. Yet I did not think of death as hard. I see no reason why a true man should fear any physical evil. What he must fear is moral slackness—moral canker! ... It is certain that no *good* action ever dies. It all seemed so vivid to me last night, and a great peace came over me as I lay and thought, and then with the sound of the guns growing fainter, I fell asleep. *(To a friend)*

In one sense, even in this dug-out, I am living life to the full, for I can cheerfully endure hardship, in fact, scorn to think of it as such, and when in danger I am not afraid.

I am so glad to have your letters. The more I see of the desolated homes out here the more thankful I am that there is a snug little home for me in England. I hope that soon I may be "on the train that's bound for Blighty." Through it all I know that your prayers are constantly going up to the Throne of Grace on my behalf, and that is a great help and cheer to me. Don't be at all anxious about me. I am very well and happy, and *I do not forget.*

A bit too tired to tell you the news. ... I often wonder what the future holds for us all in these awful days.

Don't talk of the hardship of a soldier's life. It is nothing at all, only a change from the ultra-comfortable life we used to live to a very rough and ready one. One can wash as well in a pool as in a neat bathroom, and the ground is as soft as a bed when one's as tired as I was this morning when we turned in at 2 a.m. ... The greater trial is for you at home, and the war comes hardest upon the mothers.

I am now a mile or two behind the line after having been in fairly close quarters with Fritz for a little over a week. I am doing duty at the 'phone to-night, and as things are quiet I have time to write. I am afraid my letters convey very little to you, and I wish I could tell you all I feel, but there's the censor, and one does not care to have one's intimate communications scanned by a stranger's eye. But in thinking over the events of the last few days, I feel a great sense of contentment, and thankfulness to God, and to you, for faith in God, and good health, and for that training that makes a man prefer death to dishonour, and helps him at all times to play the game. But you cannot conceive how I am longing to see you all again; and truly this is no life for a human being. It makes me cry, "How long, O Lord, how long?"

I am afraid that you will have been watching for the post in vain for "overseas" letters for the past few days, but I am writing as often as I can. We have just had four days in a trench we call "cabbage" (oh for a plate of that excellent vegetable now!); and four in another called "crump". While up there I got a lovely letter from you, M— dear. Arrived here about midnight, soaked through, having fallen headlong on the march back; when my old football ankle gives way I fall like a log. However, I managed to peg along quite well. One does not find out in times of ease of what the human mind and frame are capable, but it is good to find that with depressing conditions comes a cheerfulness of spirit which I could not have believed possible. I am supremely happy.

My life is in another's keeping, and all is well.

I'm afraid that you have lost your boy. Whenever I come back, if God spares me, I shall come back a man; and if it should be otherwise, you will know that I shall go as I have tried to live of late, as a Christian and a gentleman.

Almost everything we come into contact with is tainted by man's vices, dear A——. You must not expect to find satisfaction in purely earthly things; but remember, also, that you can make things much less hard for those around you by your own bravery and kindliness. "He never errs who sacrifices self."

When this is all over and I come back, I shall put my arms round your neck and say: "M— dear, I am *so* tired!" just as though I was little M—.

Yet you need not be anxious. I have the peace which comes from above, and have never felt the least afraid since I came out here.

… I am drawn closer to Him, and have faith to believe when things are beyond my feeble comprehension.

We are nearing the end of our stay in a wee village behind the lines, where we have no need to carry a gas mask all day. I have had a nice time and am ready for anything, which is, perhaps, as well, as a little bird has told us that we are going to a place where there is no rest for the weary, but where many a weary one has gone to his rest.

I think that you must have been thinking of and praying for me at 1 a.m. this morning. Once or twice I was afraid that you would not address any more letters to my platoon; in fact it looked as though there would be no No. 10 Platoon to address them to. We were out on a carrying party, and when we got back, our officer said that he thought we'd agree that we had all been exceedingly fortunate. It was 3 a.m. when we lay down on this concrete floor, and it felt just like a feather bed, and the next I knew, it was 10 o'clock and breakfast ready.

Sixteen of us sleep in a sort of tunnel with an exit at both ends. It is about 7 ft. wide, 25 ft. in length, and 5 in height. First I put my waterproof sheet down, then wrap myself round with my overcoat, feet in a couple of clean sand-bags, and my tunic up over my head as protection from the feet of patrolling rats.

A battle-stained company of a famous regiment marched past. If I had not been able to see the familiar badges I should have known them for something more than a line regiment, and I eagerly looked for some friends of my training time. I was rewarded by seeing — a fine big farmer and Christian. I think he looked the happiest man of the lot.

About twenty of us, Christian men of the H.B. and C.G.'s, met in the corner of a meadow for a Bible reading last night.

News from the Front

This last letter was dated Oct. 4th, and then silence until Oct. 25th, the first anniversary of his joining the Army, when there came the following letter, which had been sent to the Lady Superintendent of the Soldiers' Home at Windsor:

> Household Battalion,
> B.E.F., France,
> Oct. 16th, 1917.

"... It is with deep sympathy I convey some very sad news to you. Tpr. Mawson has not been seen by any of his comrades since Friday, Oct. 12th. He is believed to have been killed by a shell while going over. This is all I have heard concerning him, but am enquiring into it more. Would you be able to write to his people for me and break the news to them; also to other Windsor people. With much sympathy from his many friends in this Battalion."

Memories of Charlie

This letter was followed by these others from his comrades and friends, and they are given here with one purpose only, namely, to show on the testimony of other young men, who are keen judges, that the grace of God can enable a Christian young man to live so happily and wisely before others as to gain the respect and affection of his comrades.

"Charlie was a very great friend of mine in the H.B.'s.

We were attached to the 12th Division as support during the attack over some miles of frontage, and were moved about from one place to another, staying about two days at each place, when we had the order that we should go into action the next morning at 5.30—day-break. Charlie was attached to Headquarters, the same as myself, only that he was signalling and I carrying despatches from the front line to Battalion Headquarters. On the same evening we were shelled by the enemy, and Charlie was hit with a small piece of shrapnel on the right side of the head, not serious enough for him to be sent to the dressing station. His head was bandaged up and he had to 'carry on'. The next morning the barrage opened, and we went over the top all together, and reached our first objective with slight losses. It was there that we had a very rough time, and where Charlie was killed by a shell. I did not actually see him killed, but was informed that a shell burst quite close to him, killing four of them. It was talked about by everyone, as he was very popular."

"I met one of the H.B.'s and asked him if he knew Charlie. He said, 'Yes, he took me to a meeting in Windsor. He was a real Christian, with a smile and kind word for everybody.'"

"I have lost my best Christian chum."

"Charlie was a friend of mine. He was a Christian and a gentleman, every inch of him."

"We have received the following from Trooper A—, who is at the front.

'I very much regret to have to tell you that poor Mawson was reported killed last week. I cannot at present find out definitely. I have since heard very seriously wounded, but I fear the former is the case. I am very sorry indeed.'

A— became acquainted with Charlie at our house, and like all of us who knew him, held him in very high esteem. We who had the privilege of a close acquaintance with him feel his loss very much indeed. 'The righteous is taken away from the evil to come, he shall enter into peace', express much that applies to him."

"As I interpret the news that we have heard, I feel that there is no doubt that dear Charlie is even now in the presence of the Lord; and, far from these earthly scenes of strife and sorrow, gazes even now upon the glorious face of that dear Saviour whom he loved and served down here."

"It was a sad time for me when your son left for France. We had many blessed times together, and I had learned to love him. Your heart would have warmed to hear him take our daily meeting at the Home, and preach the Gospel in the neighbouring village of D———."

"It was occasionally that I was able to see and talk with him, which was a great pleasure to me, for he could sympathise with me in all my failings, being as he was a more experienced believer. On one occasion in the trenches I asked him if he found, like all Christians, that it was hard to be always rejoicing in the Lord? and he said, 'Yes, but we all have a secret peace of mind, haven't we? for God is with us.'"

"On the 4th he attended a Bible Reading among the H.B. believers on I Cor. i., and afterwards had a good talk with me."

"My youthful days seem ended on that battlefield in France, for it is seven years since Charlie and I first became friends. I remember all the joyous, laughing bathes we had together, and the world seems so much smaller now.

"Charlie prayed for me, and his prayers are answered. Never have I met God so face to face. I have found a wonderful peace, and, God be thanked, there is great consolation in Christ and His promises. It breaks down all the pride of intellect and finds a humble and contrite heart.

"In our walks together we often touched on solemn matters, and, speaking of death, I can see him now as he repeated with characteristic feeling those lines of Tennyson's:

> 'Sunset and evening star,
>   And one clear call for me;
> And may there be no moaning at the bar,
>   When I put out to sea.'[16]

"It is well with his soul, and if he could speak to us now he would only beseech us to follow the Master more closely and put our whole trust in God. I have been singing that beautiful hymn all day:

> 'O Love, that will not let me go,
> I rest my weary soul on Thee;
> I give Thee back the life I owe,
> That in Thy ocean depths its flow
>   May richer, fuller be!' "[17]

"For whether we live, we live unto the Lord; and whether we die, we die unto the Lord: whether we live therefore, or die, we are the Lord's. For to this end Christ both died, and rose, and revived, that He might be Lord both of the dead and living."—*Romans* xiv. 8, 9.

"Behold the Lamb of God, which taketh away the sin of the world."—*John* i. 29.

"Jesus said, 'I am the door: by me if any man enter in he shall be saved, and shall go in and out, and find pasture.'"—*John* x. 9.

> "Just as I am, the love I own,
> Has broken every barrier down;
> Now to be Thine, and Thine alone,
> O Lamb of God, I come."[1]

Abbreviations used

B.E.F.	British Expeditionary Force
B.G.	Beech Grove Hall, Newcastle
C.G.	Coldstream Guards
D.O.	Dug-out
D.S.O.	Distinguished Service Order
H.B.	Household Battalion
L.G.	Life Guards
L.S.W.	London and South Western (railway)
M.O.	Medical Officer
R.C.	Roman Catholic
S.A.	Salvation Army
S.H.	Soldiers' Home
S.S.	Sunday School
S.S.&S.	Sacred Songs & Solos

References to people

[a] Hedley Vicars (1826-1855): a British Army officer and evangelical who was killed in action during the Crimean War.

[b] Handley Carr Glyn Moule (1841-1920):
    evangelical theologian, writer and poet;
    Bishop of Durham (1901-1920)

[c] Duncan Matheson (1824-1869): Scottish evangelist

[d] Brownlow North (1810-1875): English evangelist

A— (on page 32):
    his sister Alice, later Mrs Alice Chambers.

M— (on pages 27, 32): his youngest sister.

References to authors

[1] Charlotte Elliott (1789-1871)

[2] Frederic W H Myers (1843-1901)

[3] T R Dale

[4] Horatius Bonar (1808-1889)

[5] Gerald Massey (1828-1907)

[6] Frances Ridley Havergal (1836-1879)

[7] Anna Lætitia Waring (1823-1910)

[8] Elizabeth Cecilia Douglas Clephane (1830-1869)

[9] Jessie Brown Pounds (1861-1921)

[10] after Mary Gardiner Brainard (1837-1905)

[11] Sidney Collett, author of "The Scripture of Truth",
London: S. W. Partridge & Co., 1908

[12] Dorothy Greenwell (1821-1882)

[13] Henry Alford (1810-1871)

[14] Sarah Doudney (1841-1926)

[15] Reginald Heber (1783-1826)

[16] Alfred, Lord Tennyson (1809-1892)

[17] George Matheson (1842-1906)

Scripture References

[†] Romans 3:15-17: [15] Their feet are swift to shed blood: [16] Destruction and misery are in their ways: [17] And the way of peace have they not known:

[‡] 1 Chronicles 12:8, 32-33, 38.

I AM KEPT

Other Books from Scripture Truth Publications

UNDERSTANDING THE OLD TESTAMENT SERIES:

HOW TO OVERCOME BY JOHN T MAWSON
ISBN 978-0-901860-62-0 (paperback)
144 pages; April 2009

DELIVERING GRACE BY JOHN T MAWSON
ISBN 978-0-901860-64-4 (paperback)
ISBN 978-0-901860-78-1 (hardback)
192 pages; March 2007

UNDERSTANDING CHRISTIANITY SERIES:

"WAITING FOR THE COMING" BY JOHN T MAWSON
ISBN 978-0-901860-67-5 (paperback)
130 pages; February 2011

CONCERNING HIMSELF BY JOHN T MAWSON
ISBN 978-0-901860-92-7 (paperback)
170 pages; March 2014

Lightning Source UK Ltd.
Milton Keynes UK
UKOW01f2040270917
309987UK00001B/14/P